AF226003

MINE.

MINE.

THE CREATOR CEO CODE

Kristina Liburd

MINE.: The Creator CEO Code

Published by Sugarcane Inheritance

www.sugarcanebooks.com

ISBN 9780999225998

First Edition, 2026

Table of Contents

SECTION III

THE REBUILD

For my husband and my children — you are the legacy

I do this for.

This is MINE.

THIS IS NOT YOUR LITTLE MOTIVATIONAL BOOK.

This is not about manifesting abundance.

It is not about stepping into your power.

It is not about hacking an algorithm.

If that's what you're looking for, there are shelves full of books that will happily sell you that.

This book is about ownership.

Not the aesthetic of it. Not the language of it. The structure.

Most creators are not failing because they lack talent, discipline, or ideas. They are losing because they do not own what they build.

You can trend and not own.

You can scale and not own.

You can sell and not own.

You can be visible and still be replaceable.

Visibility is not leverage.

Revenue is not ownership.

Applause is not protection.

If you do not control the rights, the terms, the distribution, and the escalation path when something breaks, you do not control the asset. And if you do not control the asset, you are participating in someone else's ecosystem on someone else's terms.

That is not an insult. It is a structural reality.

Ownership erodes in three places: in the platform illusion that trains you to measure momentum by attention instead of control; in contractual leakage, where urgency replaces scrutiny and rights move quietly; and in mindset complicity, where growth begins to feel synonymous with surrender.

None of those are personality flaws. They are conditioning.

You are not confused.
You have been conditioned.

This book will not comfort you about that.

It assumes you are capable of intellectual honesty — that you can examine your own agreements, your own patterns, your own tradeoffs.

It assumes you can consider the possibility that some of the rules you've internalized were not built with your ownership in mind.

What it offers is diagnosis.

If you are willing to read this carefully — not quickly, not defensively, not looking for shortcuts — you will see exactly where leverage has been leaking.

What you do after that is yours.

No one will chase you. No one will shame you. No one will beg you to care.

I will tell you the truth as clearly as I can.

The rest is your decision.

Whether you own what you build
will determine what survives you.

Those are the stakes.

If you're still here, turn the page.

Introduction

To be blunt, most creators don't own shit.

In a world where clout is measured in engagement, followers, and trends, most of it is noise. What creators actually own is permission — temporary permission from a platform to be visible according to its algorithm. They do not own their followers. They do not own the trends. They do not own the engagement. Meanwhile, they have done the labor of building user-generated platforms that grew into billion-dollar empires.

This isn't about talent. It's about ownership.

Ownership gets lost on three levels: platform, contract, and mindset.

Consider Therese, a creator who turns her creativity into a business.

First, she loses at the platform level — the platform illusion. She's told visibility equals stability. That a few cents per million views is generous. And what she isn't encouraged to read — deep in the terms and conditions — is language that gives the platform control over the content she made.

Still, she grows.

Then she loses at the contract level — contractual theft. A brand notices her. The offer is exposure or a one-time payment for her intellectual property. The payment is inadequate.

Because it will feel like a win.

She signs.

And here is what this book won't pretend it doesn't know: some of you reading this are Therese.

And you knew.

You knew the deal was thin. You knew the rights were broad. You knew the number was low. You signed anyway — not because you were conditioned, not because you didn't under-stand your worth, but because understanding your worth and being able to act on your worth are two different problems. The gap between them is often just money. Time. Options you didn't have yet. Rent due on the first. A check that clears now versus leverage that pays later.

That is not the same failure as not knowing.

This book addresses both. But it sees the difference.

If that's where you've been, this book moves forward with you.

Most creators give away rights for one of two reasons: they didn't fully understand what they were signing — or they understood and felt they had no viable alternative. In both cases, the long-term upside is sealed off in writing. The few lightning-in-a-bottle moments worked years to create are treated as disposable — when in reality they have longer shelf lives, leverage, and multiple uses.

But before either of those losses, Therese entered the economy with the third — mindset complicity.

If she understood that her business is built on intellectual property, she would treat it like an asset. She would not trade recurring leverage for a one-time check. She would build systems that compound instead of chasing algorithm highs.

Instead, she accepts the system as normal.

If Therese's path feels familiar — if you recognize decisions you're trying not to repeat — this Code was written for you.

The creator economy is a misnomer. A real economy requires exchange. This system is extractive. Platforms extract attention. Brands extract rights. Both rely on creators misunderstanding their value.

Social media didn't invent this problem. It industrialized it.

Platforms didn't create exploitation. They scaled it.

When I say "creator," I'm not just talking about social media personalities.

I'm talking about anyone whose income depends on intellectual property.

Writers. Designers. Photographers. Educators. Filmmakers. Developers. Artists. Researchers. Anyone whose work can be copied, reused, licensed, extracted, or diluted once it leaves their hands.

This is not a legal guide.

Before contracts or templates, we address the lost threads: platform illusion, contractual theft, and mindset complicity. Tools in the wrong mindset simply become weapons that backfire.

This Playbook protects what you're building: your mindset, your vision, your long-term viability.

Because let's be real: longevity has a price. This is the cost of building it.

The Ownership Gap

The ownership gap is the lie you didn't know you were living inside.

You believe what you built is yours because it feels like yours. Your account. Your audience. Your growth. But every one of those sits behind a gate you do not control — a platform, a studio, a brand, a client.

That's the gap.

You were told success meant visibility. That if you figured out the algorithm, landed the deal, hit the numbers, you had made it.

When it was over, you owned nothing.

Visibility is attention. Leverage is control.

The offer of visibility almost always comes wrapped in a quiet trade: long-term control for short-term exposure.

If nothing remains when the platform shifts, you built on borrowed land. You can decorate it, paint it, throw a party in it — and still feel the ground give way.

You are exhausted because nothing compounds. Because nothing compounds, nothing works for you while you sleep. Nothing continues earning when you stop producing. You have to create the magic every single time because you sold the first spell too cheap.

And before you say, "Well, that's just how the industry works," pause.

The industry works this way because the people at the top benefit from it working this way. Brands, studios, and platforms stack ownership. They build asset libraries. They think in decades. Meanwhile, you're told to move fast and sell cheap because life be lifing and you have bills to pay and this might be your only shot.

Scarcity drives the conditioning.

You're taught seats are limited. Attention is rare. Opportunities vanish. If you don't take the deal, someone else will.

So you move fast. You sign fast. You don't want to be difficult.

Speed benefits the party with structure.

And the math here is not about taxes. It's not about whether the check clears.

It's about longevity.

Ownership lasts your entire life plus seventy years. That's structural. When you give it up too soon, too cheaply, you are not just selling work. You are transferring future derivatives, future licensing, future leverage in rooms you haven't even entered yet.

You are mortgaging optionality.

Optionality is the asset.

You are not confused.

You have been conditioned. Conditioned to believe visibility is the prize. Conditioned to believe asserting rights makes you difficult. Conditioned to believe size determines value. Conditioned to believe that if you don't take the deal, someone else will.

That ends here.

This book closes the gap. It teaches you what you actually control, what you actually own, and what you are unconsciously giving away.

If you are willing to sit inside that tension — if you are willing to confront the possibility that some of your past decisions were shaped more by conditioning than by strategy — then continue.

Now we reset.

SECTION I

THE CONDITIONING

CHAPTER 1

Platforms Are Distribution, Not Destiny

For many creators, the platform has become the whole point. It's where they live. It's where they grow their numbers. It's where they chase likes, comments, and shares, hoping those metrics eventually translate into brand deals, validation, or stability.

That one major mistake. And it comes from misunderstanding.

Platforms are distribution tools. Period. They are a way to get your work in front of people. They are not your business. And they should never be the only place your work exists.

The story creators are told is that visibility is success. That if the numbers are high enough, everything else will fall into place.

Visibility just means you were seen.

Leverage is what you can do after someone sees you.

When your income and identity are tied to visibility alone, your foundation is unstable by design. It spikes when the algorithm is kind. It disappears — or is quietly silenced — when it's not. If your business depends on a system you cannot audit, cannot meaningfully appeal, and do not control, you do not have a foundation. You have exposure. More accurately, you have risk.

Free distribution is what made this confusing in the first place. Platforms trained creators to believe that access to an audience is enough. Post more. Optimize more. Chase reach. Very little attention is paid to what happens after the content circulates.

God forbid a creator exercise ownership rights.

Even now, as more players enter the creator economy to extract value from creators' creativity, centering ownership is quietly discouraged. Wanting control over how your work is used gets framed as being difficult. A diva moment. Ownership gets treated like an elusive upgrade instead of the point.

Being at the mercy of an algorithm isn't a platform failure. The platform is doing exactly what it was built to do. It's a marketing tool. The failure happens when a creator mistakes a marketing channel for their business model.

And the cost isn't just financial. It's emotional.

Watching one piece of content take off while another disappears. Feeling suppressed without explanation. Seeing certain topics or types of creators consistently favored while others are buried.

Over time, that instability feeds burnout, quietly squashing creativity the world may never see — not because the creator lacks talent, but because the system was never designed to support creator longevity.

If platforms disappeared tomorrow, most creators would panic. Not because their work has no value — but because nothing was built to survive without the feed. That panic is a signal. The business was never anchored.

The reason creators emotionally identify with their platform is not complicated. It's dopamine.

It is an ego hit of the highest order to watch numbers climb. When a post performs, when you trend, when you hit 100,000 views or cross a million likes, it feels like proof.

Proof that you are brilliant. Proof that you are chosen.

Proof that you are not one of the many who tried and failed.

And when you've been conditioned your entire life to believe that only the best survive, that only a few get through, that success is scarce and fleeting, that kind of validation becomes addictive.

So of course it's hard to let go.

And this isn't just social media. If you get validation through a studio picking up your script, through press coverage, through a consulting feature in a major publication, the same mechanism is at play.

If YouTube disappeared tomorrow, more than half of the creators on that platform would feel like they lost their identity. Not just their income. Their identity. They didn't just build a channel. They became "a YouTuber." They flash the plaques. They build their brand around the platform's validation. The dopamine becomes indistinguishable from ownership.

Cold eye. Calculating eye.

The platform owns the data. The platform owns distribution. The platform owns audience access. The platform owns the monetization rails.

Everything routes through them.

You are allowed to operate inside the ecosystem, but the ecosystem is not yours.

You might own your name. Maybe. If someone else hasn't claimed it first.

You might think you own your audience. If the only way to reach them is through the platform itself, you don't. That's rented access. That's standing in someone else's building hoping they don't change the locks.

And let's be honest about "community." A comment section filled with strangers, trolls, casual viewers, and algorithm-fed passersby is not ownership. If you cannot reach those people directly without asking permission first, you do not control the relationship.

That is the biggest lie about building on social.

Creators think they own something there.

They don't.

When platforms shifted from connection to retention, everything changed. The goal stopped being "connect people" and became "keep people." And to keep people, you dangle possibility. You dangle reach. You dangle monetization. You dangle fame. Dependency sets in.

Now creators obsess over algorithms. Anxiety rises when engagement dips. There is constant pivoting just to stay relevant. The plot gets lost.

Platforms were meant to be visibility channels. That's it.

You build with a platform when you use it as distribution.

You build on a platform when your business dies the moment the algorithm changes.

If your business dies when the algorithm changes, then you are working the fields for your overseer. That might sound harsh, but it's accurate. Because your dependency grew their ecosystem, not yours.

Algorithm literacy is not business literacy. Knowing how to trend is not the same as knowing how to build an asset. Knowing how to hack reach is not the same as knowing how to control leverage.

Imagine if platforms weren't "free." You would calculate differently. You would measure return differently. You would make sure that the energy you pour in produces something you can actually keep.

It has never been free.

You've just been paying in ownership.

Let's be clear - ownership is not a shield against collapse. Platforms fail. Markets shift. Categories die. Creators who did everything right have still watched environments change faster than any structure could absorb.

Discipline does not guarantee survival.

What it does is reduce avoidable loss. It ensures that when the environment changes — and it will — you still possess the asset.

The rights.

The archive.

And the optionality to rebuild somewhere else, on different terms, without starting from zero.

Ownership does not eliminate risk. It changes the odds. That is not a small thing. It is the difference between a setback and an erasure.

CHAPTER 2

Content Is Output. Brands Are Assets.

Platform equals distribution. Done.

That's not the problem.

The problem is what you're choosing to build inside of it. Is it a factory that requires constant labor or a library that compounds over time?

We know volume is rewarded. Post regularly. Stay active. Feed the machine and you might get visibility. But when volume becomes the strategy, the work shifts. You stop creating because you are inspired. You create to maintain reach.

The question shifts from *What do I stand for?* to *What does the platform want today?*

That is the turn.

The creativity that drew you to this work in the first place gets drowned out by performance metrics. That is when creators stop being owners and start becoming laborers. That is how brands get diluted, stunted, left with no growth trajectory beyond the feed.

A durable brand is not built for an algorithm. It is built for people. It is built when an audience looks for you intentionally — not because you trended, not because you gamed a sound, but because your work delivers something they return to.

Most creators do not start there. That's fine. Growth is not always fast. Brand clarity takes time. Finding your voice takes time.

The problem is not slow.

The problem is direction.

The lie is that you can chase the high first. That you can lead with junk, grab attention, and clean it up later. That once you "make it," you can go back and build something meaningful.

That reset rarely happens.

If you train the system on junk, you will keep producing junk — not because you lack depth, but because the system has been conditioned to reward the wrong thing. The work was never meant to live beyond the feed. It was built for extraction, not longevity.

When expression collapses into extraction, you become interchangeable. Forgettable. Replaceable.

At that point, there is no viability off-platform. No leverage. No compounding.

Flip the model and everything changes.

Create something once with depth and intention, then monetize it repeatedly. Platforms become tools instead of destiny.

Content is output. Your brand is infrastructure.

Content is the visible artifact — the video, the script, the post, the design. Your brand is the ecosystem: the ownership structure, the rights posture, the system that determines what happens to your work after it exists.

Acquirers only care about output. Brands want the video. Studios want the script. Platforms want the clip. They do not care about your ecosystem.

So you start believing the piece is the business.

It is not.

Content solves today's visibility. It might solve today's cash flow. It does not solve ownership. It does not compound unless you build the structure for it to do so.

When a creator says, "I just need to post more," that is factory thinking. That is laborer thinking. That is cog thinking. It is walking into someone else's system and believing speed equals safety.

You are a cog.

And emotionally, that is exhausting.

Because while you are chasing output, someone else is building assets. While you are worried about daily performance, someone else is building a library. While you are refreshing metrics, someone else is compounding value.

If you stop producing for thirty days and everything collapses, you were never building an ecosystem. You were feeding a machine.

What should stand when you pause is your own structure — something that continues to work even when you are not on the line.

A compounding creator business looks like a controlled library. Assets that can be reused, licensed, repurposed, structured, leveraged more than once. Work that can be monetized in multiple ways. Control that allows one piece of output to generate value repeatedly.

As a tactic, that might mean licensing an asset for a defined term and renewing it. It might mean allowing multiple acquirers access to the same core asset under different agreements. It might mean building derivative works from a single intellectual property foundation.

The point is choice.

Choice is leverage.

You should be in a position where you can decide whether it makes sense to sell something outright at the right number or retain control and allow it to generate value repeatedly. That position does not happen by accident. It is built.

Consistency is not asset building. Posting daily is not asset building. Viral is not asset building.

If there is no system determining how output is owned, protected, reused, and monetized, you are not building property. You are performing.

Building a business on personality instead of property is dangerous. Personalities change. Audiences shift. Relevance fades.

Intellectual property lasts longer. Controlled assets. Structured rights.

Property can be licensed. It can be inherited. It can be leveraged in rooms you have not entered yet.

But let's be clear.

Ownership does not guarantee growth.

Some assets never take off. Some ideas land in silence. Markets move. Tastes shift. The thing you built with intention can still stall.

Ownership is not a promise of return.

It is a seat at the table when the return arrives.

If the asset resurfaces — in a different market, a different moment, a different context you could not have predicted — retained control means you are still in the room. Still holding the terms. Still able to decide what happens next.

That is the difference.

Distribution is a tactic. Assets are strategy. Content is output. Brands are assets.

One keeps you on the factory floor. The other builds your library.

Ownership does not promise growth.

It promises you are still holding the keys when growth comes.

CHAPTER 3

If It Dies With the Algorithm, You Never Owned It

If you've gotten this far, something in you is reacting.

That quiet tightening in your chest. That defensive voice saying, *No. I built this.*

And you did.

You labored over it. You lost sleep over it. You refreshed dashboards at midnight. You cried over comments. You tied pieces of your identity to every milestone. Every spike. Every badge. Every "we'd love to work with you."

So when I say you don't own what you think you own, the question hits immediately:

Then what was it all for?

If that question makes you uneasy, that's not weakness. That's revelation.

Panic reveals where you placed your security. And that security was never in ownership.

It was in verification badges. Press coverage. Platform plaques. Monetization dashboards. Your foundation was built on a mountain of applause.

And applause is wind. It sounds powerful. It lifts you for a moment. But it cannot hold weight.

If your reach drops and panic follows — if engagement stalls and your chest tightens — if revenue dips the same week visibility does and you feel exposed — that's not volatility. That's dependence.

When your income depends on whether strangers happened to see your work that day, in a system built to prioritize retention, shareholders, and its own survival, stability was never the point. You were allowed to participate. You were never meant to control it.

And when the numbers dip — and they already have — the illusion cracks.

Your audience was never yours.

You appeared on a feed. Someone paused. Then they scrolled.

They weren't looking for you. Not because people are malicious. Not because your work lacks value. But because discovery was never about you. It was about entertainment.

If your business depends on repeatedly landing in front of strangers who were never seeking you, instability isn't surprising. It's structural.

That's why burnout feels existential. Unavoidable. It's not just exhaustion. It's ownership failure in disguise.

When your reaction to a drop in reach is panic, your identity fused with distribution. When your worth spikes because metrics jump, numbers became your mirror.

And when that mirror cracks, something in you resists.

You don't want it to be true. You don't want to admit that what felt solid was conditional. You don't want to believe that years of work were built on borrowed ground.

If you feel anger at that realization — if you feel defensive, irritated, even betrayed — that isn't ego.

That's grief.

Grief for the version of yourself who believed visibility was security.

Grief for the time spent sprinting toward milestones that didn't transfer.

Grief for the illusion that applause would compound into protection.

Not because the work didn't matter. But because the structure underneath it was never designed to hold you.

You were taught that success is scarce. That if you are chosen, you say thank you and don't ask questions. That if you negotiate, you're difficult. If you assert your rights, you're greedy.

So you learned to be grateful for access.

Even when access cost you control. Even when access required you to move fast, sell cheap, and smile while doing it.

You've been measuring yourself by someone else's scoreboard. And now you're realizing something uncomfortable.

If everything disappeared tomorrow — the account, the reach, the dashboard — you would have to start over.

That's the moment the illusion loses its grip.

—

You might feel angry. You might feel embarrassed. You might want to argue with me.

Good.

Because once you face the truth that nothing compounds unless you structure it to, something else becomes clear.

You can build differently. You can build portability instead of dependence.

Assets instead of applause. Systems instead of sprints.

You can bring your core audience into spaces you control. You can work with partners who respect rights instead of penalizing you for asserting them.

You can stop building for attention and start building for longevity.

Copyright lasts for your lifetime plus seventy years. That is not poetic. That is structural. Creative labor was never meant to evaporate at the end of a news cycle.

You were never meant to be disposable.

You were meant to be an owner.

End of Section I

What you've just confronted is the illusion. The validation. The numbers. The applause that felt like ownership but wasn't.

Chapters 1 through 3 were about breaking the spell.

Now we move into structure.

Revelation without mechanics collapses under pressure. Inspiration does not survive a contract dispute.

Section II is where power actually moves. In contracts. In leverage. In licensing. In protection. In the clauses that decide who controls the future and who sold it for a check.

You can't unknow what you now know. So the only question left is this:

Are you ready to build like an owner — or are you still negotiating like someone asking for permission?

That's grief.

Grief for the version of yourself

who believed visibility was security.

Are you building like an owner

or negotiating like someone

asking permission?

SECTION II

THE LEVERAGE

Pillar One: Compensation

License the Value

Let's clarify a foundational point that gets missed early and often: there is a difference between getting paid and getting compensated.

Getting paid is transactional. You perform labor. You receive a check. The exchange ends.

Compensation is different. Compensation recognizes that you created value you own, and that others want access to that value over time. When someone wants to use what you created, compensation reflects either the full realized value of that asset — or the continued value it generates through ongoing use.

Those are two different lanes.

In one lane, you are a laborer. In the other, you are an asset owner.

Labor exhausts. Assets compound.

Labor is finished when the task is complete. An asset continues to produce value. Its demand can increase. Its applications can expand. And when access to that asset becomes more valuable, the compensation tied to it should expand as well.

This is where most creators get tripped up — especially around flat fees.

Flat fees are not inherently wrong. The problem is that most flat fees are incorrect. And nine times out of ten, the person who loses is the creator.

When a brand offers a flat fee, what they often mean is this: they want to pay once and take ownership of the asset. The amount is usually too low. The rights being requested are far too broad. The creator walks away with a check. The brand walks away with long-term control.

That is backwards.

The correct lane is permission, not transfer. When a brand wants to use your work, they should be asking for permission. That permission is a license. A license defines how your asset can be used, for how long, in what manner, and on which platforms.

Ownership stays with you.

There was a creator whose work centered on family. Not spectacle. Not trends. Intimacy. She had an eye for capturing moments that couldn't be staged twice.

A brand approached her to use one of her photographs in a major advertising campaign. Real placements. Real visibility. A billboard.

The check felt enormous. It was the biggest one she had ever received. Two extra zeros compared to anything she'd been paid before. She thought she won.

She hadn't licensed the image.

She had transferred it.

All rights. Full ownership. Permanently.

It wasn't until later — after overhearing a conversation no one in her circles was having — that the realization landed. She could never use that image again. She could never license it. She could never build on it. She couldn't even revisit it for her own work.

The value wasn't gone. The ownership was.

And when the work performed — when it resonated, became recognizable, drove revenue — the upside compounded for the brand. They reused it. They extended it. They extracted value across platforms, campaigns, and time.

She started over.

Forced to recreate lightning because she sold the bottle.

The irony is this: once that same creator learned to license instead of sell, the numbers changed immediately. Four zeros became the floor. Not because her work got better — but because her posture did.

That shift is not cosmetic. It is structural.

Flat fees thrive on scarcity thinking. The belief that this might be the only opportunity. That you should be grateful someone noticed you. That if you don't take what's in front of you, nothing else is coming.

That belief is wrong.

And it's expensive.

When you accept flat fees without understanding reuse, you are not just underpricing content. You are underpricing time. Shelf life. Future leverage. You are selling tomorrow to solve today.

Ownership should change hands only when the value has already been fully realized many times over — and then some. Anything earlier requires a number so high it replaces years of upside. Not rent money. Not validation money. Exit-level money.

Because once ownership is gone, the ceiling drops. Quietly. Permanently.

For many creators, even asking for this feels foreign and out of their depth. And that's not accidental. Platforms have trained creators to treat their work as disposable, endlessly replaceable, and valuable only in the moment it performs. That conditioning has carried into negotiations.

Over time, brands have become economically dominant in these conversations. Creators have been reduced to "influencers," framed as people chasing clout rather than producing assets. That framing is deliberate. It lowers perceived value. It discourages negotiation.

So when a creator shows up asking to license their work, brands balk. They act as if negotiation is unnecessary.

Pause for a moment.

Look at what is actually happening.

The brand is seeking work. You already created it — or have the capacity to create it. The value originates with you.

If you do not believe that — if you still see yourself primarily as labor — no contract language will save you.

This is not just a drafting problem. It is a posture problem.

When you treat the check as the finish line, you relax too early. You see the metrics and assume value has been realized. You confuse performance with ownership.

You overvalue metrics and undervalue reuse.

That cognitive error is why so many creators feel like they are constantly working and never compounding.

A single asset can be licensed in different ways. Maybe it's for thirty days. Maybe it's limited to a specific territory. Maybe it's confined to one platform. Maybe it expands across multiple platforms. Each expansion of use increases the value. Each added right increases the price.

One asset, multiple revenue paths — that is compounding.

Compensation is not about getting paid once.

It is about retaining ownership and structuring access so the same asset can generate value again and again.

Content is output. Compensation is structure. License the value.

Keep the asset.

CHAPTER 5

Pillar Two: Clarity

Read the Paper Before It Costs You

It's astonishing how many smart people sign contracts they don't understand.

Not because they're incapable. Not because they're careless. But because they assume the paper is fixed. That what's in front of them is standard. That everyone is getting roughly the same deal.

For many creators, this is their first business. There's a level of naivete that comes with that. And brands are more than willing to take advantage of it.

You can't defend what you don't understand.

Creators assume the contract can't be challenged. That asking for a redline will make the deal disappear. That requesting time to review will mark them as difficult. That sending it to a lawyer will scare the brand off.

Sometimes the deal does disappear.

That's information. It tells you what kind of partner you were dealing with in the first place.

When a creator signs a work-for-hire agreement, they often don't realize what it actually means. It transfers ownership. Completely. The other party becomes the legal author. Your asset is no longer yours. Not partially. Not conditionally. Entirely.

Ambiguity always benefits the party who understands the paper. That party is usually not the creator.

Clarity is not about being adversarial. It is about positioning. Positioning yourself to protect your money. Positioning yourself to protect control. Positioning yourself to protect your time.

Fear distorts that positioning. Fear of losing the check. Fear of being labeled difficult. Fear of being replaced.

Confusion gets mistaken for compliance.

Clarity gets labeled as resistance.

That line of thinking is backwards.

And the creators who say they didn't want to rock the boat are usually masking something else — fear of being replaced. Fear that this is the only shot. Fear that another creator will take their place.

What they don't see is what happens behind closed doors.

The creator who does ask questions isn't getting replaced.

They're getting more. More money. More time. More control. Behind closed doors, brands negotiate when they want something.

They negotiate for distribution rights. They negotiate for usage expansion. They negotiate for exclusivity. They negotiate for price reductions.

They negotiate when they care.

When a creator comes to the table clear about ownership, scope, time, and use, the dynamic shifts. The brand doesn't panic. The brand engages.

Clarity is filtration. It separates partners who respect structure from partners who rely on confusion.

The most dangerous word creators overlook isn't complex legal jargon. It's "perpetual."

Perpetual doesn't mean long.

It means forever.

The deal you thought was temporary binds you years later. The license you assumed expired never did. And when your brand evolves — when you want distance, rebrand, reposition — the paper remains.

You don't reclaim that easily. You pay for it. With money. With concessions. With silence.

And sometimes, the cost isn't financial at all.

Being nice on paper costs creators control. And control is the thing that hurts the most to lose.

Money stings once.

Control bleeds for years.

There was a creator known for humor. Observational. Sharp. Her audience trusted her because she felt real.

A beauty brand approached her with a sponsored trip. Not because she was a perfect fit, but because another Black creator had already declined the deal after discovering she was being paid significantly less than her white counterparts.

The brand needed a replacement. Quickly.

She said yes.

The internet understood what had happened before she did.

The backlash wasn't about jealousy. It was about clarity. About scarcity. About stepping into a slot created by under-payment and pretending it was neutral.

She didn't pause. She lashed out.

Followers left. Creator relationships fractured. Brands watching from the sidelines saw something they avoid at all costs: instability.

Not because she lacked talent — because she looked easy to reposition. Easy to swap. Easy to burn.

There is another layer to that story that cannot be ignored.

The cost of asserting ownership is not evenly distributed. Replacement cost is not the same for everyone. When you are one of few who look like you, sound like you, or come from where you come from, walking away from the only offer on the table carries a different weight.

Scarcity shows up in more than one form. Economic scarcity compresses your choices. Social scarcity does the same. When the room is not built with you in mind, being labeled "difficult" lands harder. The margin for error narrows. The pressure to be agreeable increases.

The current runs hotter for some people than it does for others.

That pressure is real.

And it is precisely why structure matters.

If the penalty for pushing back is higher for you, then clarity cannot be optional. Terms cannot be casual. Ownership cannot be something you negotiate from inside a power imbalance without preparation.

The more asymmetric the room, the less you can afford to rely on personality, goodwill, or being liked.

Structure is not rebellion.

It is insulation.

Which is exactly why what's written on paper matters.

This is what creators misunderstand about paper: it doesn't just govern money. It governs perception.

Being known as "easy" closes doors quietly. Brands remember who reads. They remember who questions. They remember who folds.

Nothing changes the dynamic faster than a creator who says, calmly:

This contract doesn't work. I need these terms changed. I'm sending this to my lawyer. I need a license instead of a transfer. I need clarity on scope and time. I need to understand what I'm agreeing to.

That is not aggression. That is structure.

Trusting implicitly is not a strategy.

Cutting through the bullshit with clarity is.

CHAPTER 6

Pillar Three: Control

Ownership Is Optionality

Ownership is not fleeting.

A one-time payment is.

That's the distinction people blur because the check feels immediate and ownership feels abstract. But abstraction doesn't mean weakness. It means horizon.

A payment has a ceiling. Ownership doesn't. Unless every dollar you've ever collected is compounding at the same exponential rate that retained rights can, there is always a limit to what that payment can do for you.

Ownership insists on itself.

Ownership is control. And control is far more valuable than certainty.

The certainty many creators think they need is the check. The quick hit. The relief of "if I get this payment, I'm good." Life be lifing. Bills are real. Pressure is real. I'm not pretending otherwise.

But relief runs out.

Control doesn't. Control creates optionality.

Optionality means people have to come back to you. Optionality means access is not assumed — it is granted. Optionality means you are not negotiating from desperation, smiling while doing it, hoping they don't notice you need this more than they do.

And here is the irreversible moment: the second you convince yourself that your ownership isn't that serious — that it's not worth protecting, that you can always recreate the work — you've crossed a line you may not be able to walk back. That's when it's functionally gone.

Imagine what happens when access to what you built requires your permission every single time.

Think about any major tech company. Pick one. It doesn't matter which. Their ownership has compounded for decades. Their name signals value before a product is even announced. They don't scramble for relevance. They don't beg for placement. The leverage is embedded in what they control.

Now imagine operating like that.

Where your name carries weight. Where people know what you create has value before you open your mouth. Where access requires terms.

Compare that to giving it up at the drop of a hat because the number felt big in the moment.

It looks cheap.

And I know you're not cheap.

When you retain ownership, the posture changes.

You stop asking for a seat at someone else's table. This is your table now. You decide who comes. You decide when they come. You decide how much access they get. Maybe it's thirty days. Maybe it's six months. Maybe it's one territory. Maybe it's global. Maybe it's exclusive. Maybe it's not.

You set the boundaries.

Control sets the tone before numbers are even discussed.

Ownership is not a shield against collapse. Platforms fail. Markets shift. Categories die. Creators who did everything right have still watched environments change faster than any structure could absorb. Discipline does not guarantee survival.

What it does is reduce avoidable loss. It ensures that when the environment changes — and it will — you still possess the asset. The rights. The archive. The optionality to rebuild somewhere else, on different terms, without starting from zero. Ownership does not eliminate risk. It changes the odds. That is not a small thing. It is the difference between a setback and an erasure.

Creators have been conditioned to prioritize short-term security because long-term leverage makes other people uncomfortable. If creatives are optimized for convenience — speed, dopamine, quick wins — they're easy to exploit.

If creatives are optimized for control, the entire equation shifts.

The losses from early ownership transfers are quiet. They don't announce themselves. No alarm sounds. The well just narrows. The field just shrinks. Opportunities don't explode — they thin out over time. And you don't always realize it until you're staring at work that should have paid you again and never will.

But I can point to creators who understood control early — and watched everything compound because of it.

One creator I worked with operates in one of the loudest spaces imaginable: travel. Everyone is visible. Everyone is pitching. Everyone thinks reach is the prize.

What set her apart wasn't output. It was discipline.

She treated ownership as sacred. She didn't scatter her rights across one-off deals. She paid attention to where her assets lived and who had access to them. She didn't move fast just because the check cleared fast.

Once her audience stabilized, brands didn't come to her for content.

They came for access.

That's different.

Social media turned into magazine features. Features turned into a book. The book turned into an app. One asset became derivatives. Derivatives became a system.

That shift didn't happen because she was louder. It happened because she was structured.

Her name became the asset. When major brands came calling, there was no scrambling. There was clarity. She knew what she would license. She knew what she wouldn't. And brands adjusted to her posture.

This is what control does.

It changes who chases who.

When you walk into rooms thinking you should be grateful to be there, people treat you accordingly. When you walk in knowing what you own, people straighten up.

Now let's talk about the objection.

"That's a long game. I've got bills."

I know.

But what you're actually buying with a guaranteed check isn't safety. It's relief. Relief from negotiating. Relief from uncertainty. Relief from standing your ground.

That relief expires.

And when it does, you're back at the beginning, hoping you can catch lightning again.

That's not strategy. That's gambling.

And gambling feels productive right up until it isn't.

Here's the warning again: the belief that you can always recreate what you gave away is seductive — and wrong. Even if you later make enough money to try to buy it back, you're paying to recover something that should have remained yours. By the time you realize what you lost, it's been reused, diluted, embedded somewhere you can't easily unwind.

Ownership works differently.

The moment you create something, it's yours. The only way someone takes it is if you sign it away. When you lead with that posture — this is mine — the tone shifts before money ever enters the room.

Ownership does the negotiating for you.

Think about Charlie and the Chocolate Factory.

The golden ticket wasn't just access. It was leverage. It changed Charlie's position before he ever stepped inside. It separated him from the crowd. It gave him standing. And ultimately, it positioned him to walk away with the entire factory.

The ticket didn't work because he begged. It worked because he had it.

Ownership is the golden ticket.

You cannot cross this.

This is mine.

Period.

So come correct.

Lose ownership, and the first thing you lose isn't money. It's leverage.

And once leverage erodes, negotiations shrink. Pricing shrinks. Options shrink. After enough short-term wins, the well dries up. The magic fades. The work doesn't hit the same.

Regret is quiet at first — then it's loud.

You were never meant to be a disposable cog chasing checks to stay afloat.

You were meant to control what you build.

And once you understand that ownership is optionality, you stop negotiating for survival.

You start negotiating from power.

CHAPTER 7

Protection Is a System, Not a Panic Response

If ownership is the golden ticket, protection is how you keep it.

Nine times out of ten, creators only start thinking about protection when shit has already hit the fan. Something got taken. Something got reused. A takedown notice shows up. An infringement notice shows up. Or worse — they realize they don't actually know what they agreed to in the first place.

Protection almost never feels urgent.

Until it is.

And by then, you're not preserving leverage. You're negotiating damage.

I've watched creators spiral in that moment. Every email feels loaded. Every call feels like it could make things worse. They don't know who to call. They don't know what applies. They don't even know where their own boundaries are. So they react. Under pressure. At someone else's pace.

That's panic-based protection.

Protection shows up late. Always late.

And when it's late, the cost isn't just money. It's leverage. It's narrative control. It's reputation.

Audiences are ruthless about this. They don't care how reasonable you are. They care who looks like they're scrambling. Once you're scrambling publicly, you're not in control of the story anymore. You're defending it.

Now let me show you the contrast.

There's a creator I've worked with for years. Things have gone wrong for her too — because things always go wrong when you're building something real. But I have never seen her panic.

Not once.

Not because she's fearless. Not because she's lucky. But because she built systems before she needed them.

She knows her contracts. She knows who reviews her paper. She knows where her assets live and who has access to them. She knows what she controls and what she doesn't. So when someone crosses a line, she doesn't spiral.

She enforces. Quietly. Quickly.

No public meltdown. No frantic Instagram stories. No confused audience trying to piece together what happened. Chaos never touched her because her system spoke for her.

That's the difference.

One creator is reacting to risk. The other designed against it.

Protection isn't about paranoia. It's about leverage preservation.

When it's baked into the foundation of your business, it does something most creators don't expect.

It gives you freedom.

Real freedom.

The freedom to create without second-guessing whether you own what you're building. The freedom to enter relationships knowing where the lines are. The freedom to say yes, no, or not yet without fear because you already know what's yours.

Psychologically, it changes how you move.

You don't flinch when pressure hits. You don't overexplain. You don't fold because someone sounds official in an email. You already know where you stand.

I tell creators to think of protection like a bulletproof vest. You don't put it on after the shot is fired. You wear it so you can walk into rooms differently. You negotiate differently when you know the core of your business is protected. You don't lead with fear. You lead with structure.

And still, I hear the same things.

"I'll deal with it later."

Later is where leverage goes to die.

"It's too early for that."

No. What you mean is something else feels more important right now.

A better camera. A bigger set. More polish. More visibility.

Here's the truth.

A studio-grade camera will not stop someone from infringing your work. A beautiful feed will not protect your reputation.

A bigger audience will not save you if you don't know what you've already given away.

Systems do that.

Knowledge is power. Infrastructure is power. Protection is power.

When protection is foundational, it shapes everything. It informs your minimums. It clarifies your non-negotiables. It makes it very hard for anyone to pull the wool over your eyes because the baseline is already set. You know what's yours. You know what you'll accept. You know what crosses the line.

And that clarity preserves leverage long before conflict shows up.

Now let's be clear about something else.

Doing too much is also a mistake.

Not everything needs an NDA. Not every idea needs to be locked down. Not every early-stage creator needs dense, overbuilt contracts for deals they aren't even doing yet.

Overprotection is what happens when fear drives the build instead of clarity. Fear will choke your business just as fast as negligence will.

The goal isn't maximum protection.

The goal is appropriate protection — protection that matches where you are now and doesn't collapse when you grow.

A real system scales. You know what you rely on today. You know what comes next. You recognize when you've outgrown your setup before you're in the middle of a crisis.

Creators who treat protection as a reaction don't just pay financially.

They pay with their peace.

First their peace. Then their money.

Because when protection is reactionary, you're always behind. Always catching up. Always explaining yourself. Always trying to claw back something that was easier to secure at the beginning.

Protection done right doesn't look dramatic. It looks boring. It's almost invisible. It stops feeling heavy. It stops feeling scary. It starts feeling like what it actually is — the thing that lets you move fearlessly and build something that lasts.

Ownership gave you optionality. Protection keeps it intact.

Reacting to risk feels busy.

Designing against it preserves power.

CHAPTER 8

Stage-Appropriate Protection

If protection is infrastructure, it has to match the structure it's supporting.

There are stages to this.

Early.

Growth.

Scale.

The risks shift. The leverage shifts. The pressure shifts. Protection has to shift with it.

Most creators treat protection like a light switch — on or off — instead of a system that evolves. And that's how things start bending.

Early

Some early-stage creators don't think protection applies to them because they don't think they have anything worth taking.

I'm just starting out.

Nobody's looking at me.

I'm not making real money yet.

They confuse low visibility with low value.

Value doesn't begin when attention shows up. It begins the moment something is created.

The first time that belief cracks is usually when the work gets bigger than expected. A contract with more moving parts. A deal that feels real. More money than they've ever seen. Suddenly there's something on the table — and now there's something that can be taken.

That's when the paper starts ruling how you partner. How you create. How you associate with brands. And you realize you agreed to more than you understood — not because you were careless, but because you outgrew what you had in place.

But here's the correction.

Overprotecting too early can be just as harmful as under-protecting too late.

At the beginning, the goal is clarity, not excess.

If other people are working alongside you, contracts matter. Ownership needs to be clear. Anything created in connection with your brand should revert back to you. If you're naming your brand, clearance matters. You don't build equity only to discover you have to rebrand because someone else got there first.

That's the baseline.

Not maximum protection.

Appropriate protection.

You don't need dense, overbuilt agreements for things you aren't even doing yet. You don't need to trademark every idea before the market has proven demand. You don't need to paper every casual conversation like you're negotiating a merger.

If your business pivots — and many do — you don't want to have sunk time and money into protecting something that never mattered.

Early stage protection is about anchoring ownership and leaving room to move.

Growth

Growth changes the equation.

Once visibility increases and reuse starts showing up in conversations, new risks emerge. Brands want more. Partners want expanded rights. Your work starts moving in ways you didn't anticipate.

This stage comes with friction. That's a normal growing pain. The problem isn't the strain. The problem is ignoring it.

Many creators assume the primary risk here is theft.

Often it's not.

The risk isn't failure.

It's erosion.

Boundaries get crossed quietly. Ownership gets fuzzy. Deliverables multiply. Rights expand because nobody pushed back the first time.

And it doesn't look catastrophic.

It looks like success.

More deals. More inbound. More visibility.

Which is exactly why creators stop paying attention.

This is where licensing literacy becomes essential. Not just conceptually — structurally. You need to understand what's being asked of you. You need to recognize expanded usage. You need to know when a one-time fee is quietly turning into perpetual access.

Volume becomes the stressor.

Too many requests. Too many conversations. Too many agreements moving at once.

That's usually the first signal you've outgrown your original setup.

The system starts to strain. Reviews take longer. Decisions feel rushed. You're still wearing every hat because that's how you've always done it.

The risk isn't dramatic collapse.

It's slow dilution.

What feels like control is actually drag.

You're overseeing more and creating less. You're approving instead of building. And without upgraded infrastructure, that oversight isn't sustainable.

That's not failure. That's leverage thinning out in real time.

Scale

When you hit scale, the rules change again.

You're no longer just a creator. You're a brand others rely on. Teams depend on you. Partners depend on you. Platforms recognize you. Your audience expects consistency.

At this stage, protection stops being about individual contracts and starts being about systems. Tracking usage. Knowing when licenses expire. Ensuring trademarks are actually filed once the business has proven itself.

Managing multiple assets that now carry reputational weight.

Now protection compounds instead of constrains.

And now the standard shifts.

Not having your paper in place isn't a mistake.

It's negligence.

Confusion becomes expensive. Confusion about who owns what. Confusion about who does what. Confusion about how assets are managed. Confusion about how your name is used.

When creators try to skip stages, things break.

They waste money on systems they don't need yet. Or they avoid upgrading until responsibilities collapse because nothing is anchored. Leverage cracks. Reputation takes a hit. And the foundation starts to show stress fractures that are hard to hide later.

You can recover from some of it.

But cracks always cost more to repair than to prevent.

This stage stretches muscles most creators have never used before. Not creative muscles. Leadership muscles.

You can't hold every thread anymore. You can't review everything yourself. You can't rely on memory and goodwill. If you can't step away without things wobbling, your system was never built to scale.

What feels like control is actually drag. And drag slows everything.

Protection that doesn't match your stage doesn't fail loudly.

It fails by slowing you down — until the business starts running you instead of the other way around.

—

You'll usually know you've outgrown your setup before anyone else does.

You're stressed. Burned out. Doing too much. Holding every decision because letting go feels risky.

That's not strength.

That's a signal.

Protection isn't static. It shifts as you shift. The goal isn't perfection. It's proportion. It's responsiveness. It's reinforcing the system before pressure turns into fracture.

That's how protection stays powerful.

End of Section II

So here it is.

No more pretending. No more sticking your head in the sand.

You don't have an overseer forcing you onto a factory line. You have platforms. You have partners.

You have ecosystems built on your labor.

And if you've read this far — if you know what happens when protection doesn't match your stage, if you know what happens when leverage thins out, if you know what cracks cost — and you still operate the same way?

That's not conditioning anymore. That's consent.

Because now you know.

Section III is where the posture changes.

Because knowing the math is one thing. Living like a CEO is a motherfucker. It's harder. It's slower.

It requires restraint when your ego wants validation.

It requires patience when your bills are screaming.

It requires discipline when a brand dangles a shiny check in your face.

It requires you to stop performing and start leading.

Up until now, we've exposed the illusion. From here forward, we build.

This is no longer conditioning.

This is consent.

Because now you know.

SECTION III

THE REBUILD

CHAPTER 9

AI, Reuse, and the Myth of "Too Small to Matter"

If protection is infrastructure, this is the terrain it has to survive.

AI doesn't care about your visibility. It cares about availability.

That's the shift most creators still haven't metabolized.

Part of the failure is psychological. It's easier to perceive a threat when there's a face attached to it — a competitor, a company making a direct ask, a person you can argue with. A machine feels neutral. Helpful, even.

And that's exactly why it's dangerous.

For years, the comfort story has been that being small is a kind of protection. Nobody's looking at me. I don't have anything worth taking. I'm just one voice in a crowded feed.

But AI doesn't evaluate fame. It evaluates access.

If your work is available, it's useful. If it's useful, it's valuable. And if it's valuable, it will be taken — quietly, incrementally, and at scale.

Extraction doesn't begin with the famous. It begins with the exposed.

Small, unguarded pockets of the internet are exactly where systems thrive. That's where the raw material lives.

Pretending you're invisible doesn't make you safe.

It makes you easy.

The pattern didn't begin with machines. It began with humans.

Someone reposts your content. Remixes it. Lifts it. Maybe a larger account does it and it feels flattering. Maybe the platform even encourages it.

But it's still reuse you didn't explicitly consent to.

That's the first boundary people learn to ignore.

Then it escalates. Word-for-word copying. Identical formats. Your voice, your structure, your work stripped of attribution and reposted like it's public domain.

What feels like flattery is extraction.

AI removes the human friction from that same pattern. "Inspiration" becomes a catch-all excuse. A system ingests your work, generates something adjacent, and no one can clearly say who owns the output — which conveniently dilutes ownership of the original in the process.

Systems move faster than consent. Faster than attribution. Faster than enforcement.

The point of no return isn't theft.

It's normalization.

Once reuse stops looking like a violation and starts looking like progress, the leverage has already shifted. And that framing benefits everyone except the creator.

This is why titans negotiate early.

When companies like Disney partner with platforms and technology firms, they aren't reacting out of panic. They're responding from leverage. They built systems before the threat arrived. They drew lines around their assets before someone else did it for them. They negotiated licensing structures and usage parameters while they still had the weight to enforce them.

At scale, they can throw that weight around.

Smaller creators don't get to throw weight around in the same way. But the principle isn't different. The asset may be smaller. The logic is identical.

Build the system before the threat metastasizes.

If you wait until extraction feels obvious, you're already negotiating damage.

The framing most people get stuck in is pro-AI versus anti-AI. That's not the real question.

AI has legitimate uses. It creates efficiency. It unlocks productivity. Leverage doesn't come from ideology. It comes from systems.

Being anti-AI doesn't stop scraping. Being pro-AI doesn't create consent, attribution, or respect. Those things don't come from opinion. They come from infrastructure.

Opting out sounds comforting, but it's mostly performative. It's the same fantasy as posting disclaimers and pretending platform terms don't apply. AI isn't one system. It's thousands. Opting out of one while the rest continue scraping is a game you cannot win.

The damage isn't dramatic.

It's cumulative.

And what actually gets absorbed isn't trend-based content or throwaway posts.

It's your language. Your ideas. Your vernacular. Your tone. Your way of explaining things — the parts of your work that are distinctly human.

Those are the most dangerous once they're absorbed, because you understand their nuance and the system doesn't. It reproduces them without context, without restraint, without regard for how they were meant to live in the world.

Once that originality is diluted and made mainstream, you don't lose it entirely.

You lose your edge.

The thing that once differentiated your work becomes harder to defend — not because it disappeared, but because it's everywhere. That's irreversibility.

Not theft. Normalization. And this cuts both ways.

In an AI-driven world, seeking permission matters more, not less. It signals how you operate. It tells people whether you respect creative labor or exploit ambiguity. It shows whether you expect others to treat your work with care because you do the same.

The system reflects what you normalize.

Opting out of free reuse adds value. Choosing not to make your work endlessly available trains the market how to treat you. It removes the signal that you're easy, that you're grateful for exposure, that anything you create is up for grabs.

Scarcity, when intentional, strengthens ownership.

And pretending you don't matter won't save you.

CHAPTER 10

When Giving Up Ownership Is Strategic

Ownership is not a religion.

It is doctrine. And doctrine only works if you understand when it serves you — and when you serve it.

Up to this point, we've argued that maintaining ownership is usually the right move. Usually. That word matters. Because strategic exit is not the opposite of ownership discipline. It is the fullest expression of it.

The creator who knows when to release an asset without flinching is the creator who understood its value long before the negotiation began.

There are situations where giving up ownership makes sense. They are rarer than people want to admit, but they exist.

The cleanest example is work with no afterlife. It was built for one person, one use, one moment. There is no meaningful reuse market. No secondary audience. No derivative expansion. The asset dies when the job ends.

In that case, holding ownership does not create leverage. It creates overhead.

But the math does not change.

You are still giving something away that, by default, belongs to you for your lifetime — and seventy years after that. You are not just transferring a file. You are transferring optionality. The right to decide what happens next. And once ownership is gone, you don't get a vote.

So conditions have to be met.

Not in a checklist way. In a consequence way.

The labor has to be paid at a level that reflects permanence, not just hours worked. The emotional toll has to be acknowledged if the work required identity, reputation, or exposure. The speed the buyer is purchasing — their ability to move without you — has to be priced. The reach they could unlock, even if you never intended to take it there, has to be factored in. Geography. Derivatives. Continuation.

Because the buyer is not just buying the work.

They are buying the future versions you will never get to make.

There are very few industries where creators retain meaningful power after a full transfer. Residuals exist in some corners of entertainment — but those are exceptions with their own histories, unions, and rules. For most creators, once it's sold, it's gone. No derivatives. No continuation. No second bite.

That is why selling ownership only works when there is nothing left for you to take from the asset.

No further aspiration. No expansion path. No speed advantage you could unlock yourself. No derivative future you actually want.

This is the furthest it will ever go — and you are being paid accordingly. Anything short of that is not strategy.

It is calling exhaustion a business decision.

One of the clearest ways to tell whether you are making a strategic exit or acting out of desperation is how you feel about the check.

If you are itching for it. If you are rushing. If you are skipping questions because you are tired, broke, burned out, or simply ready to be done.

That is not strategy. That is exposure.

A strategic exit feels different. It slows down. It calculates. It forces you to articulate what leverage survives the transfer.

I tell my transactional skills students that every negotiation requires a floor. What are you absolutely not willing to give up? If that line is crossed, you walk. Regret rarely comes from walking away. It comes from caving under pressure and realizing years later that you surrendered something you cannot recover.

If you cannot name your floor before the negotiation begins, you are not making a strategic decision. You are reacting.

Longevity sharpens this calculus.

Ownership does not cover your working years. It covers your life. And then it covers the people who come after you. We are still talking about artists and writers who have been dead for decades whose estates are still eating off the fruit of their labor.

That is not romantic.

That is math.

So if you are going to sell, the number in your head almost never cuts it. Not once you factor in time, reach, and everything downstream.

There are rare moments when letting go costs less than holding on. When the window is short. When the idea dies on impact. When policing ownership becomes another asset you do not need to manage. In those cases, freeing the bandwidth allows you to focus on work that compounds.

But understand what is being purchased.

The buyer is buying speed. Scale. Risk removal. Derivative rights. The ability to move without asking you.

And if you sell ownership without preserving leverage somewhere else, control evaporates with it.

That distinction matters more now than ever — especially in an AI-driven environment where likeness, voice, and identity can be reused at scale. Chapter 9 made that clear. If your name, face, or creative signature can travel faster than consent, the structure of your deal is the only thing standing between stewardship and dilution.

This is why the Khaby Lame deal matters — not because of the headline number, but because of the structure.

In early 2026, he sold his company in a deal valued at roughly $900 million. The number is impressive. It is also irrelevant if you do not understand what happened underneath it.

He did not confuse visibility with value. He diversified partnerships. He allowed the business to mature independently. He licensed his likeness — including for AI use — in ways that preserved control rather than surrendered it. Expansion without erasure.

And when the company sold, he did not disappear.

He rolled ownership forward.

He retained a controlling stake in the acquiring entity. Control did not evaporate at exit. It transformed.

But here is the detail most people glide past:

It was an all-stock deal.

No immediate liquidity. No guaranteed payout. No clean walkaway.

Equity does not buy certainty. It buys continued exposure — to performance, governance, and long-term stewardship. You do not leave the risk behind. You carry it forward.

Nobody desperate for a check structures a deal that way. That is chosen risk, not fled-to certainty.

Cash buys distance, often at the cost of influence.

Equity buys influence, often at the cost of time and exposure.

Neither is morally superior. Both are tools. The mistake is entering either without clarity about what you are preserving.

Strategic exit is not surrendering ownership doctrine. It is applying it so precisely that you know when release strengthens your position instead of weakening it.

If you cannot point to the leverage that survives the transfer, you did not execute an exit.

You conceded one.

CHAPTER 11

Cash Now vs. Control Later

Cash solves today.

Control shapes tomorrow.

That's the trade.

And the most expensive lie creators tell themselves when choosing cash is this: there will always be more later.

Say it out loud and you can hear how fragile it is. The adult version of believing money grows on trees. The idea that there will always be another buyer. That your output will stay consistent. That your momentum is permanent.

Human consistency tells us otherwise.

Markets change. Energy changes. Timing shifts. And financial pressure has a way of distorting judgment until the deal in front of you feels like the only deal you'll ever get.

This is where the real shift happens. It's not about strategy. It's when life starts screaming.

Bills are loud. Responsibilities are loud. Time feels short. And suddenly the long game feels irresponsible.

I need to get paid.

I can't wait for this to compound.

Fuck my descendants. I'm living now.

That thought is more common than anyone wants to admit. And it's not evil. It's human.

Sometimes Cash Now is not greed. It's oxygen. It's buying yourself out of panic. It's choosing stability over hypothetical leverage because hypothetical leverage doesn't pay childcare.

There is no moral failure in that choice. But there is a cost. And the cost compounds quietly.

So the check gets framed as practical. Reasonable. Necessary. What it's actually buying is emotional peace.

A short hit. The anxiety quiets. You breathe again. Maybe the relief lasts weeks. Maybe months.

And then it wears off. That's when the regret curve begins.

Not immediately. Almost never immediately. It shows up later — when the asset resurfaces in your mind. When you want to use it again. When you realize you can't. When someone asks for a version of the thing you already made and you shut yourself out of the conversation because the rights are gone.

What creators rarely calculate is the outlier scenario. The possibility that the work you poured yourself into becomes the thing. The thing that scales. The thing that compounds. The one you sold for pennies that turns into millions for someone else.

There is nothing more painful than watching upside you once held turn into someone else's leverage.

That regret isn't dramatic. It's slow.

It's like speeding on a highway.

For a while, it feels great. You're flying. You don't trust the next opportunity is coming on its own, so you go faster. Faster. Faster.

And then there's a sharp turn you didn't calculate for.

You don't have room to slow down. You don't have the control to adjust. You crash — not because the road was unfair, but because speed replaced foresight.

Speed replaced foresight. And foresight is leverage.

Control works differently.

Control gives you options when the road bends. It lets you slow down. Re-route. Even stop if you need to. It doesn't mean you move slowly forever. It means you're not reckless with the future.

None of this means you shouldn't get paid. This is not a binary. It never was. You can get paid and retain control. You can structure money over time.

You can negotiate royalties, equity, licenses, staged payments, shared upside.

Urgency feels like agency. It feels like survival. It feels like maturity. But urgency is exactly what extraction systems rely on.

They want you anxious. They want you tired. They want you grateful for the guaranteed check. Because once you move too fast, they don't have to negotiate. They don't have to share upside. They don't have to come back.

The system wins the time game.

It always has.

Before you sign, ask yourself three things.

1. Ask whether this is a decision you can live with later.

2. Ask whether you're trading relief for regret.

3. Ask whether you're giving up control because it's strategic — or because you're tired.

The all-stock structure in Chapter 10 wasn't a financial technicality. It was a refusal of urgency. It was a decision to carry risk forward rather than eliminate it for immediate certainty.

That posture is available at every level — not the $900 million level, the psychological level.

Choosing cash over control doesn't just cost you options. It mortgages the future. And once it's sold, there's no refinancing.

The system has always relied on you not thinking that far ahead.

Now you do.

CHAPTER 12

DIY vs. Tools vs. Escalation

Creators escalate when confidence collapses.

That's the moment. Not when the contract gets complicated. Not when the stakes increase. When confidence cracks.

DIY doesn't start as recklessness. It starts as bravery. You feel capable enough to try, and you don't have the money to outsource. Sometimes it's one. Often it's both. That part is normal.

Where it turns is ego.

Ego disguises itself as control. And control disguises itself as responsibility.

The structure of that disguise is the problem. Each layer is legitimate on its own. Control is real. Responsibility is real. Ego uses both as cover.

But what's really underneath is fear.

Fear of cost. Fear of admitting you're out of depth. Fear of letting someone else see how the business actually runs.

DIY becomes self-protection dressed up as discipline.

In the early stages, doing it yourself makes sense. Resources matter. Confidence matters. You don't need a team for your first small deal. You don't need outside infrastructure when revenue barely covers expenses.

Where it breaks is when DIY stops being a phase and turns into a belief system.

At some point, you know.

You know the contracts are heavier. You know the risk is layered. You know the consequences are real. And instead of escalating, you hedge.

You pull in tools.

Software. Templates. AI. Something that promises to close the gap without forcing you to admit that your competence hasn't caught up with your confidence.

Some tools help. AI can be useful as a starting point — for drafting, negotiation prep, scenario modeling.

But a starting point is not understanding.

Tools generate results. They don't explain consequences.

Ask AI for a "great contract" and it may give you something polished. Clean formatting. Familiar clauses. Confident language.

That confidence is borrowed.

If you don't know what to scrutinize, what's missing, or what's dangerous, you are carrying someone else's certainty without owning the judgment behind it.

That's how creators walk into negotiations thinking they're prepared and leave having been quietly steamrolled. Not because they weren't intelligent. Because they mistook output for insight.

Think about fire.

The breakthrough wasn't discovering it. It was learning how to contain it. One person holds a burning stick too close and gets burned. Another builds a contained flame that warms everyone nearby.

The tool didn't change. The operator's understanding of its consequences did. Access to tools does not make you wiser. It reveals how you use them.

Urgency complicates this further. Urgency feels like agency. It feels like survival. It feels like maturity. But urgency isn't judgment. It's pressure.

Platforms amplify that pressure. Not just social media — any distribution system optimized for scale. They reward immediacy. They reward visibility spikes. They reward whatever keeps eyes moving.

Low-effort attempts should expect low-effort results.

Relying on platforms or tools to do strategic thinking for you is delegation without discernment. And avoidance shows up everywhere.

You delay because you don't want to spend the money. You delay because you're afraid of scrutiny. You delay because ego tells you needing help means you failed. Every one of those delays costs you options.

Options disappear first.

The option to spend less. The option to negotiate from strength. The option to choose your partners instead of taking whoever says yes. The option to control timing. The option to protect before damage happens.

Maturity is recognizing limits.

It's understanding that you are not supposed to do everything yourself. That some things are not your strength. That some risks are not worth absorbing just to prove you can handle them.

Growth requires letting go of the Superman fantasy and finding the right person to remove the obstacle.

Escalation isn't failure. It's judgment.

The moment you escalate appropriately is the moment you stop acting like labor and start acting like leadership. From execution to oversight. From carrying risk alone to distributing it intelligently. From reacting to deciding.

Refusing to escalate isn't independence. It's self-sabotage.

Escalation is the first visible act of CEO thinking. Not because someone handed you the title. Because you finally stopped protecting your ego and started protecting your business.

CHAPTER 13

Signs You've Outgrown Your Setup

There are signs long before misalignment becomes obvious.

By obvious, I mean real damage. Lost money. Lost rights. Deals you can't undo.

But before it ever gets that far, the signals start quietly.

The first is scrambling.

You don't know where anything lives anymore. You're hunting for contracts. Digging through folders. Wondering if the final version was in a spreadsheet, an email thread, a form, or someone else's drive. Nothing is centralized. Nothing feels settled. You're always reacting instead of operating.

The second sign is scrambling to feel prepared.

And I'm not talking about brand kits or media decks. I'm talking about what's inside them — especially around rights. What you can say yes to. What you won't. What's non-negotiable. When that isn't clearly articulated, every conversation starts from zero. You're improvising instead of asserting.

Then omission creeps in.

You bring things to the table with brands, but you're missing pieces. You forget to state your terms upfront. You don't anchor expectations early. Brands should know what's on the table from the beginning. When they don't, it's usually because you don't either.

This is the moment where creators mistake chaos for success.

I'm busy, so I must be winning.

I'm in demand.

But there's a difference between controlled momentum and frantic adjustment. Growth pain feels pressured but intentional. Misalignment feels scattered.

You stop keeping score.

Contracts start coming in and you assume they're fine without tracking what rights you've already given away. You stop remembering who has access to what. You've scaled, but your pricing hasn't adjusted. That gap starts showing fast.

And then repetition sets in.

You solve the same problem over and over again and call it productivity. You tell yourself it means things are working because you've handled it before.

If you're solving the same problem repeatedly, you don't have mastery.

You have a leak.

Mastery is solving the problem once, building a system that handles it, and freeing yourself to move higher. Busyness is not scaling. Overload is not success. Being slammed does not mean you have a handle on things. It just means you're busy — and you're probably busy with the wrong shit.

Nothing has collapsed yet. But the cracks are visible. Growth without structural evolution isn't progress.

It's accumulation.

And accumulation without architecture eventually collapses inward.

You know you've outgrown your setup when you're fighting against an imaginary clock and losing.

It shows up as exhaustion. A short fuse. That constant urgent feeling like the clock is ticking and you have to go, go, go — even when nobody is actually chasing you. You can't rest without guilt because you've convinced yourself there's no time. You're behind. You're late. You're failing.

And the first place it shows up is in your mind.

Cognitive fatigue. Decision fatigue. That slow, heavy feeling where everything takes longer to process and the simplest choices start to feel like math. You push past it anyway because you've been taught mind over matter. You tell yourself you just need to grind a little harder.

But it doesn't stay in your head.

It bleeds into your body. It bleeds into your words. It bleeds into how you talk to people. You start moving like someone under pressure even when the pressure is self-made.

Then resentment starts showing up.

You get burnt out with brands. Burnt out with platforms. Burnt out with your audience. You start side-eyeing other creators who seem to be doing better than you are. You tell yourself it's jealousy.

It's not jealousy. It's misalignment.

Resentment isn't ingratitude. Resentment is often the first honest signal that your setup no longer fits you.

Not because you hate your audience. Not because you're ungrateful. It's the emotional response to a system carrying more weight than it was built for. Resentment is not a moral flaw. It's structural feedback.

You entered this because something about creating called you. Something about building with your own mind and your own hands pulled you in. If you're starting to hate the game, that's not a personality flaw. That's a structural signal.

And recognizing it is not comfort. Awareness is not comfort. It's the only window you have before the cost compounds. As long as you can see it, you still have agency.

This is the false competence zone. This is the phase where everything looks functional from the outside. You're delivering. You're earning. You're visible.

And you are quietly exhausted.

Because the system works — but it only works if you keep over-functioning inside it. You're competent enough to survive, but not structured enough to scale. And that is the most dangerous place to live because you're producing. You're getting by. Meanwhile you're stagnant — and calling stagnation stability.

The hardest stage to leave is the stage you're in.

Because you already figured it out. And moving up is scary. Moving up makes you question yourself. Am I good enough for that? Do I have the money? Do I have the resources? Do I have the systems?

So you push through. You keep grinding. You keep telling yourself you'll fix it later.

And eventually that stops working. The bottleneck shows up.

Nine times out of ten, the bottleneck is you. Everything is waiting on you because you can't execute faster without breaking. You can't decide faster because you don't have enough clarity to choose. Once execution and decisions start stalling, quality follows right behind it.

The work slips.

The communication slips.

The follow-through slips.

And then you pay the price that actually gets people's attention.

Opportunities disappear.

The door closes and doesn't reopen. The brand doesn't follow up. The collaborator stops calling. The invitation doesn't come back.

And one day you may realize that the thing you were most proud of — your opus, your signature work, your pièce de résistance — was sold for nothing because you didn't know what you were agreeing to.

Not because you weren't smart. But because you waited too long to change.

If your business cannot function without you in every decision, you don't own a system.

You own a job.

CEOs don't build jobs. They build structures.

And structures outlast the people who built them.

The Path Forward — DIY, Tools, Sprint, or Audit

You already know whether you're staying the same or not.

That's the real choice in front of you. Not which tool. Not which hire. Not which tactic. Whether you are staying the same.

The four paths in front of you are not equal options. They are postures toward reality.

DIY is the most defended posture. It works when you're early and the stakes are small, but DIY long-term is not independence — it is containment. It demands you stay small enough that your mistakes don't cost too much. Ego will tell you you can stretch it further. One more template. One more late night. One more contract you think you understand. DIY protects comfort but does not expand capacity.

Tools are the next posture. Tools solve execution problems — they speed things up, reduce friction, support a system — but they do not create one. When you lean on tools to make judgment calls for you, you tried to outsource leadership. Tools can accelerate clarity. They cannot replace discernment. They cannot replace ownership. They cannot replace you.

A sprint is different. A sprint is not just speed; it is pressure. It is a stress test for your systems. If your contracts are disorganized, a sprint exposes it. If your pricing has no floor, a sprint exposes it. If your rights are scattered across inboxes and platforms, a sprint exposes it.

DIY avoids exposure.

Tools soften exposure.

A sprint forces exposure.

And then there's the audit. An audit is not an indictment. It's a diagnosis.

It tells you exactly where the pressure points are — what's broken, what's leaking, what you're carrying that you shouldn't be carrying. It threatens the ego that kept you comfortable. It threatens the story you've been telling yourself about being fine because you're busy.

It's gonna check you, boo.

That's not cruelty. That's leadership. Because if you actually want to grow — not just accumulate, not just survive — you need reality. You need truth. You need a mirror that doesn't care about the narrative you rehearsed.

But posture alone isn't action.

Maybe you need to track what assets you've already given away so you can set a new floor moving forward. Maybe you're fine licensing rights, but you need to know which rights, to whom, and for how long. Maybe you're building an asset library and need clarity around reuse — what's licensed, what expires, who needs to stop using what or start paying you more.

These are not abstract reflections. They are Monday morning decisions.

Moving forward means putting away old things — even the ones that once worked. It means deciding that what's next deserves a different level of intention. Forget what's behind you. Build toward what's ahead.

A year from now, where are you aiming?

Not hoping. Aiming.

More control over your assets, cleaner negotiations, decisions made from clarity instead of fear — whatever it is, name it. Then decide which direction you're moving.

Toward comfort.

Or toward clarity.

You are not making decisions for this quarter. You are making decisions on a timeline that outlasts you.

Lifetime plus seventy years is not a slogan. It is the math of ownership. The systems you build — or refuse to build — determine who benefits from your work long after you're gone.

Clarity costs ego. Clarity costs comfort. Clarity sometimes costs money. Clarity is the only thing that compounds.

The wrong path isn't the expensive one.

It's the one that keeps you small.

Build Like an Owner

Ownership creates leverage. Ownership stabilizes confidence. When every decision you make is filtered through what you own and what you're protecting, something shifts. You negotiate differently. You create differently. You walk away differently. Not louder. Just steadier.

Think about the difference between renting and owning a home.

When you rent, you enjoy the space. You follow the rules. You move on when it's time. You're not responsible for the foundation, the long-term upkeep, or what happens after you leave. Someone else owns the ground beneath you.

When you build on platforms you don't control, it's the same thing. You benefit from the space, but someone else owns the foundation. They control distribution. They change the rules. And when the lease ends, so does your leverage.

Ownership is different.

When you own, you maintain. You invest. You upgrade. You care — not sentimentally, but structurally. You know where the money flows — whether that's equity, liquidity, or both — and you protect it accordingly.

The same is true for your work.

Ownership builds respect. Respect for the energy, the time, the creativity, and the resources you've poured in. When you churn content just to feed an algorithm, that respect erodes. The work starts to feel disposable because you're treating it that way.

But when you create with intention — for the people who actually care, whether that's travel, gaming, books, art, storytelling, or something else entirely — the work carries weight. And if it carries weight, it deserves structure.

Stop tolerating disrespect.

Stop accepting being rushed.

Stop pretending exposure is payment.

You put in the work. You put in the sweat. You put in the resources. There is no reason to let anyone treat your output like it's interchangeable or cheap.

I've laid out where you've probably made mistakes. You don't have to like being called out. You don't have to enjoy it. But absorb it.

Absorb that ownership is the end game.

Absorb that delay erodes leverage — quietly, while you're convincing yourself you'll fix it later.

Absorb that outsourcing judgment is not the same as outsourcing tasks.

If it scares you to change how you operate, good. Growth should.

Most creators aren't trying to win an algorithm. They're trying to build something that lasts — something that outlives platforms, outlives trends, outlives the feed.

The systems built to extract from you don't care about your intentions. They care about what's on paper, what's enforceable, and what holds when pressure hits.

That is exactly why the system you build has to be airtight.

External systems extract.

Your system protects.

Lifetime plus seventy years is not a slogan. It's the math of ownership. The infrastructure you build — or refuse to build — determines who benefits from your work long after you're gone.

Build something that protects you.

Build something that pays you.

Build something that outlives you.

About the Author

Kristina Liburd is a Creator Ownership Strategist, attorney, and the founder of the Creator CEO Playbook. For over fifteen years she has worked with creators, founders, and creative businesses on the judgment calls that happen before contracts, cash, and metrics enter the picture — the ones that determine who actually controls what gets built.

MINE. is the foundation of that work.

She lives with her husband Everett and two children Ella and Benny, for whom everything is built.

This book was the diagnosis.

The Creator CEO Playbook is where
you build the system.

If MINE. reoriented how you see your
work, the Playbook is where that shift
becomes infrastructure — the tools,
the judgment calls, and the structure
to protect what you're building at
every stage.

creatorceoplaybook.com

Build something that protects you.

Build something that pays you.

Build something that outlives you.

MINE.

www.ingramcontent.com/pod-product-compliance
Lightning Source LLC
Chambersburg PA
CBHW040037070726
47636CB00085B/639/J